The Youtube Code: The Secrets to Increasing your Audience, Views, and Revenue as a Content Creator

By

Robert D. Gibson

TABLE OF CONTENT

Introduction

The Rise of YouTube: From Platform to Cultural Phenomenon

In the ever-evolving landscape of the Digital age, few innovations have left an indelible mark on global culture quite like YouTube. What began as a simple online platform for sharing videos in 2005 has transcended its humble origins to become a transformative force, revolutionizing how we consume, create, and interact with content.

In the early days, YouTube was primarily a platform for casual video sharing, a virtual playground where individuals could upload and discover a wide array of content, from endearing home videos to quirky skits and cat memes. However, it wasn't long before the world began to take notice of the platform's untapped potential.

The pivotal moment that catapulted YouTube into the cultural stratosphere was the advent of viral videos. Overnight sensations like "Charlie Bit My Finger" and "Gangnam Style" transcended geographical boundaries, leaving an indelible mark on popular culture and showcasing the internet's immense power to connect people through shared experiences.

As YouTube's influence expanded, so too did the rise of a new breed of digital celebrities: YouTube creators. Armed with little more than a camera, a unique perspective, and boundless creativity, these individuals struck a chord with millions, earning loyal followings that rival those of mainstream celebrities.

Beyond entertainment, YouTube became a catalyst for societal change. It played a pivotal role in sparking and amplifying social movements, giving a voice to marginalized communities, and raising awareness on pressing issues. From "Kony 2012" to "Black Lives Matter" and "Me Too," YouTube served as a platform for activism, driving real-world impact through the power of storytelling and shared experiences.

The phenomenon of YouTube has not been without its challenges. As the platform grew, so did concerns around content moderation, copyright infringement, and the spread of misinformation. YouTube found itself navigating complex ethical dilemmas, balancing the principles of free expression with the need to protect its users and society from harmful content.

Today, YouTube stands as a dynamic cultural hub, a place where creativity knows no bounds, and where diverse voices find resonance. It continues to evolve, giving rise to new formats, trends, and opportunities for creators and viewers alike.

Chapter 1

Finding Your Passion

In the vast and diverse landscape of YouTube, finding your passion is the first step towards carving a niche that sets you apart from the crowd. Whether you aspire to be a lifestyle vlogger, a gaming enthusiast, a makeup artist, an educational content creator, or anything in between, understanding what truly excites you is the key to building a meaningful and sustainable presence on the platform.

Identifying Your Niche: What Sets You Apart?

In a sea of content creators, it's essential to identify a niche that aligns with your interests, expertise, and unique perspective. Your niche is your creative territory, the area where you can demonstrate your expertise and passion authentically. Begin by asking yourself a few basic questions:

- **What do you love to do?** Look within yourself and identify the activities that bring you joy and fulfillment. Whether it's playing video games, cooking, fashion, technology, or any other subject, passion is the driving force that fuels creative excellence.

- **What are your skills and strengths?** Consider your talents and areas of expertise. Are you a talented artist, a skilled coder, a great storyteller, or a knowledgeable researcher? Leveraging your skills enhances your content's value and sets you apart from others in your niche.

- **What makes you unique?** Embrace your individuality and quirks. Your authentic self is what resonates with audiences. People are drawn to creators who are unapologetically themselves and who bring a fresh and distinctive perspective to their content.

- **Who is your target audience?** Understanding your potential audience is crucial for finding your niche. Make sure your material is customized to their requirements and interests. Engaging with your viewers and understanding their preferences can help you refine your niche and content strategy.

Once you have identified your niche, commit to it wholeheartedly. Consistency and dedication are vital to building an engaged audience who appreciates your content and comes back for more.

The Power of Authenticity: Embracing Your Unique Voice

In an era of digital saturation, authenticity stands as a beacon of trust and relatability. Embracing your unique voice and sharing your authentic self is a powerful way to connect with your audience on a deeper level. Here's why authenticity matters on YouTube:

- **Building Trust:** Authenticity breeds trust. When viewers sense that you are genuine and transparent, they are more likely to connect with you emotionally and trust your recommendations and insights.
- **Relatability:** People gravitate towards content creators who they can relate to. Your authentic self allows viewers to see that you are just like them, which fosters a sense of community and belonging.
- **Standing Out:** In a crowded content landscape, being authentic sets you apart from others. Your voice and perspective are what make your content unique and memorable.
- **Longevity:** Trends come and go, but authenticity remains timeless. Being true to yourself and your passion ensures that your content has a lasting impact and continues to resonate with audiences over time.

Chapter 2

Content Strategy and Planning

Content strategy and planning are the backbone of a successful creator's journey. As Youtube continues to grow and diversify, the key to standing out and engaging with your audience lies in crafting compelling content ideas and mastering the art of storytelling.

Crafting Compelling Content Ideas

A well-crafted content idea is the foundation of any successful YouTube video. It's the hook that captures your audience's attention and entices them to click and watch. To create content that resonates with your viewers, consider the following strategies:

- **Understand Your Audience:** It is vital to understand who your target market is. Research their interests, preferences, and pain points. Pay attention to the comments and feedback you receive to gain insights into what they want to see more of.

- **Be Relevant:** Stay up-to-date with current trends and topics in your niche. Crafting content that is relevant and timely ensures that your videos remain valuable and shareable.

- **Solve Problems:** Your content should aim to solve your audience's problems or provide valuable information. Whether it's a how-to tutorial, a product review, or an informative piece, offering solutions fosters trust and establishes you as an authority in your field.

- **Collaborate and Cross-Promote:** Partnering with other creators or businesses can expand your reach and introduce your content to new audiences. Collaborations also inject fresh perspectives into your channel, keeping your content diverse and engaging.

- **Experiment and Innovate:** Don't be afraid to try new content formats or experiment with different styles. Audiences appreciate creativity and innovation, and taking calculated risks can lead to exciting discoveries.
- **Leverage Seasonal and Special Events:** Capitalize on holidays, seasons, or special events to create themed content. Thematic videos add variety to your channel and tap into the audience's festive spirit.
- **Accept Audience Feedback:** Pay attention to what they have to say and change your material accordingly. Engaging with your viewers builds a sense of community, and incorporating their suggestions fosters a stronger connection.
- **Create Series:** Developing content series or regular features provides consistency and keeps your audience anticipating your next video. Series also help organize your

content, making it easier for new viewers to discover related videos.

By crafting content ideas that align with your audience's interests and needs, you not only attract new viewers but also foster loyalty among your existing subscribers.

The Art of Storytelling: Keeping Viewers Engaged

Storytelling is a powerful tool that transcends time and captivates audiences across cultures and mediums. On YouTube, storytelling goes beyond traditional narratives; it's about creating a compelling and emotional experience that resonates with your viewers. Here's how to master the art of storytelling on the platform:

- **Begin with a Hook:** Capture your audience's attention from the start with an engaging hook. Whether it's a provocative question, a surprising statement, or an intriguing visual, the opening seconds of your video are crucial for retaining viewers.

- **Develop a Narrative:** Structure your content in a way that flows logically and keeps viewers engaged. A clear beginning, middle, and end help guide your audience through the story, creating a satisfying viewing experience.
- **Inject Emotion:** Emotions are the driving force behind memorable stories. Whether it's humor, inspiration, empathy, or excitement, evoking emotions in your audience creates a deeper connection.
- **Be Transparent and Vulnerable:** Sharing personal stories or challenges can make your content more relatable and humanize your channel. Authentic vulnerability can foster a stronger bond with your viewers.
- **Use Music and Sound:** The right background music or sound effects can enhance the emotional impact of your

story. Carefully selected audio elements can elevate the viewing experience and set the tone for your content.

- **End with a Call-to-Action:** Conclude your video with a clear call-to-action, such as subscribing, liking, or sharing. Encouraging viewer engagement helps build a loyal community around your channel.

- **Polish Your Editing:** Smooth and seamless editing keeps the story flowing and prevents viewer boredom. Cut out unnecessary fluff and maintain a good pace throughout the video.

Storytelling is a potent tool that creates a lasting impact on your audience, encouraging them to return for more engaging and emotionally resonant content.

Chapter 3

Creating High-Quality Videos

From the initial setup to the final edit, every aspect of video production plays a vital role in enhancing production value and engaging the audience. We will explore the importance of essential gear and equipment in creating professional-looking videos and the art of mastering video editing to polish your content and leave a lasting impression on your audience.

Essential Gear and Equipment: Enhancing Production Value

Investing in essential gear and equipment is a crucial step in elevating the production value of your videos. While some creators start with minimal equipment, upgrading as your channel grows can significantly enhance the overall quality of your content. Here are some essential items to consider:

- **Camera:** A high-quality camera is the foundation of professional-looking videos. While many smartphones have impressive cameras, dedicated digital cameras or DSLRs offer more control over settings, better image quality, and interchangeable lenses for different shooting scenarios.
- **Tripod or Stabilizer:** Keeping your camera steady is essential for smooth and professional-looking shots. A tripod or stabilizer helps eliminate shaky footage and allows you to create more dynamic and visually appealing videos.
- **Microphone:** As crucial as high video quality is clear and crisp audio. Investing in an external microphone, such as a Lavalier or shotgun mic, increases audio capture dramatically, reducing background noise and improving the entire viewing experience.
- **Lighting:** Proper lighting is vital for well-lit and visually pleasing videos.

Consider investing in softbox lights or LED panels to illuminate your subject and create a professional-looking setup.

- **Background and Set Design:** Choose a clean and visually appealing background or set design that complements your content. A well-thought-out background can add depth and professionalism to your videos.

- **External Hard Drive:** Video files can consume a lot of storage space. Keeping your video on an external hard drive guarantees you have enough capacity for your projects and keeps your PC functioning properly.

- **Green Screen:** For creators who want to experiment with special effects or create a more dynamic background, a green screen allows for easy background replacement during video editing.

- **Camera Bag:** A durable and well-padded camera bag protects your gear during transportation and keeps everything organized and easily accessible.

Remember that while having top-of-the-line equipment can enhance production value, the most critical aspect is how you use these tools to tell your story and engage your audience effectively.

Mastering Video Editing: Polishing Your Content

Video editing is where the magic happens. It's the process of piecing together your footage, adding transitions, effects, music, and more, to create a cohesive and polished final product. Here are some key tips for mastering video editing:

- **Select the Appropriate Software:** There are several video editing software alternatives available, ranging from beginner-friendly to professional-grade. Final Cut Pro, Adobe Premiere Pro, and DaVinci Resolve are all popular options.

Choose software that is appropriate for your needs and level of skill.

- **Organize Your Footage:** Before diving into the editing process, organize your footage into folders to make the workflow more efficient. A well-organized file structure helps you find clips quickly and keeps your editing process streamlined.

- **Create a Storyboard:** If your video follows a specific narrative or structure, creating a storyboard or outline can help guide your editing process. A storyboard acts as a roadmap, ensuring you stay on track with your storytelling.

- **Trim and Cut:** Start by trimming unnecessary footage and eliminating any mistakes or fluff. Keep your editing tight and concise, ensuring every clip serves a purpose in advancing your narrative.

- **Enhance Audio:** Audio is just as crucial as video quality. Use audio editing tools to adjust levels, remove background noise, and add music or sound effects to enhance the overall audio experience.

- **Apply Transitions Wisely:** Transitions, such as cuts, fades, and dissolves, should be used judiciously to create smooth transitions between shots and maintain a cohesive flow.

- **Color Correction and Grading:** Adjusting colors and applying grading effects can drastically change the mood and tone of your video. Color correction ensures an accurate representation of the footage, while grading adds a creative touch to evoke specific emotions.

- **Add Text and Graphics:** Incorporate text overlays, lower thirds, and graphics to provide context, emphasize key points, and reinforce your branding.

- **Pace Your Editing:** Maintain a balanced pace throughout your video. Vary the rhythm of cuts and transitions to keep viewers engaged and prevent monotony.

- **Preview and Review:** Take breaks while editing to maintain fresh eyes on your work. Preview your video multiple times, seeking feedback from others if possible, to fine-tune your content.

- **Export Settings:** Choose the appropriate export settings to ensure your video retains high quality when uploaded to YouTube. Different platforms have specific requirements, so be mindful of these settings to avoid compression and quality loss.

Remember that video editing is an art form, and each creator develops their unique style over time. Consistent practice, learning from other creators, and exploring various editing techniques can help you refine your skills and deliver captivating videos.

Chapter 4

Building and Engaging Your Audience

In the dynamic world of YouTube, building and engaging a loyal audience is the key to long-term success. As a content creator, understanding your audience, their preferences, and their needs is essential for tailoring your content and fostering meaningful connections.

Understanding Your Audience: Utilizing Analytics and Insights

To build a thriving YouTube channel, it's crucial to have a deep understanding of your audience. YouTube provides creators with powerful analytics and insights that offer valuable data on viewer behavior, demographics, and content performance. How to maximize the use of these tools is as follows:

- **Study Audience Demographics:** YouTube Analytics provides information about your viewers' age, gender, location, and interests. Understanding your audience's demographics helps you tailor your content to their preferences and create content that resonates with your target audience.

- **Track Watch Time and Viewer Retention:** Watch time is a critical metric that measures the total time viewers spend watching your content. It's an essential factor in YouTube's algorithm for suggesting videos. Analyzing viewer retention can help you identify which parts of your videos are engaging and which may lead to viewer drop-off.
- **Analyze Traffic Sources:** YouTube Analytics shows where your viewers are discovering your content, such as through YouTube searches, suggested videos, external links, or social media. This information helps you focus on promoting your videos where your audience is most likely to find them.

- **Monitor Audience Engagement:** Pay attention to metrics like likes, dislikes, comments, and shares. Engaged audiences are more likely to interact with your content and positive engagement signals to YouTube that your content is valuable.
- **Test and Learn:** Use A/B testing to experiment with different video formats, titles, thumbnails, and descriptions. Analyze the performance of these variations to understand what resonates best with your audience.
- **Address Viewer Feedback:** Engaging with your audience through comments is an excellent way to gather feedback. Responding to comments and incorporating viewer suggestions can foster a sense of community and strengthen the connection between you and your audience.
- **Use YouTube Studio Beta:** YouTube Studio Beta offers additional insights and

tools, including real-time analytics, personalized tips, and a dashboard that provides an overview of your channel's performance.

Understanding your audience is an ongoing process. Continuously monitoring analytics and adapting your content strategy based on viewer behavior ensures that you stay relevant and meet your audience's evolving preferences.

Interaction and Community Building

Beyond analyzing data, engaging with your audience and fostering a sense of community is crucial for building a loyal following. Here are some strategies for interaction and community building on YouTube:

- **Respond to Comments:** Interact with your audience by responding to comments on your videos. Whether it's answering questions, expressing gratitude for positive feedback, or addressing constructive criticism, engaging with your viewers makes them feel valued and heard.

- **Host Q&A Sessions:** Periodically host Q&A sessions where you answer questions from your audience. This personalizes your channel and strengthens the connection between you and your viewers.

- **Create Community Posts:** Utilize YouTube's Community tab to post updates, polls, and questions. Community posts encourage viewers to engage with your channel outside of video content.

- **Live Streams and Premieres:** Host live streams and premieres to interact with your audience in real-time. Live events provide an opportunity for direct communication and a more intimate connection with your viewers.

- **Create a Branded Hashtag:** Encourage your audience to use a branded hashtag when engaging with your content or creating user-generated content related to your channel. This helps create a sense of community around your brand.

- **Be Consistent and Reliable:** Consistency in uploading videos and interacting with your audience builds trust. Regularly engage with your community to keep the connection strong.
- **Recognize Your Most Engaged Viewers:** Show appreciation to your most active and supportive viewers by giving them shout-outs or featuring their comments in your videos.

Building a community around your channel takes time and effort, but the rewards are immeasurable. A loyal and engaged audience is more likely to share your content, support your channel, and become advocates for your brand.

Chapter 5

SEO and YouTube Algorithm

Getting your content discovered by the right audience can be challenging. However, understanding the YouTube algorithm and optimizing your metadata and titles can significantly improve your videos' visibility and reach.

Decoding the YouTube Algorithm: How it Works

The YouTube algorithm is a complex and ever-evolving system that determines which videos are shown to users and in what order. The primary goal of the algorithm is to maximize user engagement and satisfaction by recommending relevant and compelling content. Here's an overview of how the YouTube algorithm works:

- **Watch Time:** Watch time is the total amount of time users spend watching your videos. YouTube prioritizes videos with higher watch times as it indicates that the content is valuable and keeps viewers engaged.

- **Viewer Retention:** Viewer retention measures how long viewers stay engaged with your videos. Content that maintains high viewer retention rates is likely to receive higher rankings in search results and suggestions.

- **Click-Through Rate (CTR):** CTR is the percentage of viewers who click on your video after seeing it in search results or suggested videos. A higher CTR suggests that your video's title, thumbnail, and metadata are compelling and relevant.

- **Video Engagement:** Engagement metrics, such as likes, dislikes, comments, and shares, play a crucial role in determining video popularity and ranking. Videos with higher engagement are more likely to be recommended to a broader audience.

- **Session Time:** YouTube aims to keep users on the platform for as long as possible. Therefore, videos that lead to more extended viewing sessions or multiple video views are favored by the algorithm.
- **Relevancy and Context:** The algorithm analyzes the content of your videos, including titles, descriptions, and closed captions, to determine relevancy to user searches and preferences.
- **User Behavior:** The algorithm takes into account a user's watch history, search history, and other interactions on YouTube to personalize recommendations.

It's important to note that the YouTube algorithm's exact workings are proprietary and not publicly disclosed by YouTube. Therefore, the factors mentioned above are based on observations and insights from creators and experts.

Optimizing Metadata and Titles: Boosting Discoverability

To improve your videos' discoverability and increase the chances of appearing in search results and suggestions, optimizing your metadata and titles is essential. Here are some strategies to consider:

- **Keyword Research:** Conduct keyword research to identify relevant and popular search terms related to your content. Tools like YouTube's own search suggestions, Google Trends, and third-party keyword research tools can help you find valuable keywords.

- **Compelling Titles:** Create attention-grabbing and descriptive video titles that convey what the video is about. Use relevant keywords in the title to improve the chances of appearing in search results.

- **Thumbnails:** Design eye-catching and visually appealing thumbnails that accurately represent your content. Thumbnails are the first impression viewers have of your video, and a compelling thumbnail can entice more clicks.

- **Accurate Descriptions:** Write detailed and accurate video descriptions that provide context and information about the content. To improve search exposure, use relevant keywords in the description.

- **Tags:** Use relevant tags to further enhance your video's discoverability. Tags help YouTube understand the content of your video and match it with user searches.

- **Playlist Optimization:** Organize your videos into playlists with descriptive titles and relevant keywords. Playlists keep viewers engaged and encourage them to watch more of your content.

- **Consistent Branding:** Develop a consistent branding strategy across your titles, thumbnails, and overall channel design. Consistency helps viewers recognize and associate your content with your brand.

- **End Screens and Cards:** Utilize YouTube's end screens and cards to promote other videos, playlists, or calls to action, encouraging viewers to continue watching your content.
- **Monitor and Optimize:** Continuously monitor the performance of your videos and adjust your metadata and titles based on audience behavior and feedback.

Remember that YouTube's algorithm is continuously evolving, so staying up-to-date with the latest trends, algorithm changes, and best practices is essential for optimizing your content for discoverability and growth.

Chapter 6

Monetization Strategies

For content creators on YouTube, exploring various monetization strategies is essential for turning their passion into a sustainable and profitable career. While ad revenue is a primary income source, diversifying revenue streams and partnering with brands can significantly boost earnings and provide more stability.

Diversifying Income Streams: Beyond Ad Revenue

- **YouTube Partner Program (YPP):** The YouTube Partner Program allows eligible creators to monetize their content through ads served on their videos. To qualify for the YPP, channels must have at least 1,000 subscribers and 4,000 watch hours in the past 12 months. Once accepted, creators can enable monetization and earn revenue based on ad impressions and clicks.

- **Channel Memberships:** Channel memberships, also known as "Join" or "Memberships," allow creators to offer exclusive perks to their subscribers in exchange for a monthly fee. These perks may include custom badges, emojis, exclusive content, and access to members-only live chats.
- **Merchandise Shelf:** The merchandise shelf enables creators to showcase their merchandise directly on their YouTube channel. Viewers can easily browse and purchase merchandise, such as t-shirts, mugs, or accessories while watching videos.
- **Super Chat and Super Stickers:** Super Chat and Super Stickers are features that allow viewers to make monetary contributions during live streams or premieres. In exchange, their messages or stickers are highlighted to stand out in the chat.

- **YouTube Premium Revenue:** YouTube Premium subscribers pay a monthly fee for an ad-free experience, access to YouTube Originals, and offline viewing. Creators receive a portion of the revenue produced by YouTube Premium users who see their material.

- **Crowdfunding:** Platforms like Patreon, Kickstarter, and Tipeee offer creators the opportunity to receive direct financial support from their fans. In return, creators often provide exclusive content or rewards to their patrons.

- **Affiliate Marketing:** Affiliate marketing allows creators to earn commissions by promoting brands or services. By including affiliate links in video descriptions or dedicated promotion videos, creators earn a percentage of sales generated through their unique links.

- **Licensing and Content Syndication:** Selling licenses to your content or syndicating it to other platforms can provide additional income streams. This strategy allows creators to reach broader audiences and generate revenue from multiple sources.

- **Public Speaking and Workshops:** Successful creators can leverage their popularity and expertise to secure opportunities for public speaking engagements or workshops. These events can generate income while expanding the creator's brand and influence.
- **Educational Courses and Ebooks:** Creating and selling educational courses or ebooks related to your niche can be a lucrative revenue stream. Platforms like Udemy or Teachable offer creators the tools to monetize their knowledge and expertise.

Partnering with Brands: Navigating Sponsorships and Collaborations

Brand partnerships, sponsorships, and collaborations can be valuable opportunities for creators to earn revenue while promoting products or services that align with their content and audience. However, it's essential to approach brand deals with authenticity and transparency to maintain trust with your audience. Here are some tips for navigating brand partnerships:

- **Choose Reputable Brands:** Partner with brands that align with your values and content. Promoting products or services that you genuinely believe in fosters authenticity and enhances your credibility with your audience.

- **Disclose Sponsored Content:** It's essential to disclose any sponsored content to your audience. YouTube's guidelines require creators to disclose brand deals and sponsorships in video descriptions and, when applicable, verbally in the video itself.

- **Negotiate Fair Deals:** Negotiate fair compensation for your collaboration, taking into account factors such as the reach of your channel, engagement metrics, and the level of effort required for the promotion.
- **Create Engaging Sponsored Content:** Craft sponsored content that seamlessly integrates the brand's message while providing value to your audience. Avoid overly promotional content that may come across as insincere.
- **Long-Term Partnerships:** Forming long-term relationships with brands can benefit both parties. Consistent brand collaborations can provide stable income and allow you to create more integrated and authentic sponsored content.
- **Protect Your Brand:** As a creator, your brand is valuable. Be selective with brand

partnerships and ensure they align with your content and audience to maintain your brand's integrity.

- **Negotiate Exclusivity:** When negotiating brand deals, consider exclusivity clauses that prevent competitors from sponsoring similar content during a specific period. This can maximize your earnings from the partnership.

- **Review Products Honestly:** If you're reviewing products or services as part of a sponsorship, offer honest and unbiased opinions. Your credibility relies on providing genuine feedback to your audience.

By exploring various monetization options, creators can build a sustainable income and reduce reliance on a single revenue source.

Chapter 7

Navigating Challenges and Overcoming Burnout

Being a content creator on YouTube comes with its fair share of challenges. From facing criticism and negative comments to managing the pressure of staying creative and consistent, content creators often encounter obstacles that can lead to burnout.

Handling Criticism and Negative Comments: Building Resilience

- **Develop a Growth Mindset:** Embrace a growth mindset, which focuses on learning and improvement. Instead of viewing criticism as a personal attack, see it as an opportunity to grow and refine your content.
- **Filter Constructive Criticism:** Not all criticism is negative; some can be constructive and helpful for your growth.

Learn to distinguish between constructive feedback and unfounded negativity.

- **Engage with Positive Comments:** Respond to positive comments and engage with viewers who appreciate your content. Focusing on the positive feedback can help counterbalance the negative.

- **Set Boundaries:** Limit the time you spend reading comments or engaging with negative individuals. Setting boundaries protects your mental well-being and prevents negativity from overwhelming you.

- **Surround Yourself with Supportive Communities:** Connect with other content creators or join communities that offer support and understanding. Engaging with like-minded individuals can provide a sense of camaraderie and help you cope with criticism.

- **Remember Your Purpose:** Remind yourself why you started creating content in the first place and the positive impact you have on your audience. Staying connected to your purpose can motivate you to keep going despite criticism.

- **Report and Block Trolls:** If you encounter abusive or malicious comments, report them and block the users to maintain a healthy online environment.

Balancing Creativity and Consistency: Avoiding Burnout

- **Set Realistic Goals:** Define achievable goals for your channel and content. Unrealistic expectations can lead to burnout when you feel like you're constantly falling short.
- **Plan Ahead:** Create a content calendar and plan your videos. Planning helps you stay organized and reduces the pressure of coming up with ideas at the last minute.
- **Embrace Flexibility:** While consistency is essential, allow yourself some

flexibility in your content schedule. If necessary, adjust your posting frequency to avoid burnout.

- **Prioritize Self-Care:** Look after your physical and mental health. Prioritize sleep, exercise, and relaxation to recharge and stay creative.
- **Collaborate with Others:** Collaborating with other creators can bring fresh perspectives to your channel and relieve some of the pressure of creating content on your own.
- **Experiment with New Formats:** Trying out new content formats or styles can reignite your creativity and enthusiasm for creating content.
- **Listen to Your Audience:** Pay attention to your audience's feedback and interests. Creating content that resonates with your viewers can boost your motivation and engagement.

- **Delegate Tasks:** If possible, delegate certain tasks, such as editing or social media management, to others to free up time for creative endeavors.
- **Take Creative Breaks:** Don't be afraid to take creative breaks when needed. Stepping away from content creation for a short period can lead to renewed inspiration.
- **Seek Inspiration:** Seek inspiration from other creators, books, movies, or art forms that resonate with your interests. Inspiration can spark new ideas and fuel your creativity.
- **Be Kind to Yourself:** Be patient with yourself and acknowledge that burnout can happen to anyone. Treat yourself with compassion and avoid being overly critical of your work.

Chapter 8

Leveraging Social Media and Cross-Promotion

As a content creator on YouTube, expanding your reach and growing your audience is essential for success. Leveraging social media and cross-promotion are two powerful strategies that can significantly boost your visibility and help you connect with a broader audience.

Expanding Your Reach: Harnessing the Power of Social Media

Social media platforms offer content creators a powerful means to expand their reach beyond YouTube. By strategically using various social media channels, you can promote your content, engage with your audience, and attract new viewers. Here are some tips for leveraging social media to grow your YouTube channel:

- **Choose the Right Platforms:** Different social media platforms cater to various content types and demographics. Identify the platforms where your target audience is most active and focus your efforts on those channels.

- **Cross-Promote Your Content:** Share snippets, teasers, or highlights of your YouTube videos on social media. Entice your followers to watch the full video by providing intriguing previews.

- **Engage with Your Audience:** Social media is all about building connections. Respond to comments, messages, and mentions to engage with your followers and foster a sense of community.

- **Use Eye-Catching Visuals:** Social media thrives on captivating visuals. Use eye-catching images, graphics, and thumbnails to grab your audience's attention and encourage them to engage with your posts.

- **Schedule Posts Strategically:** Consistency is key on social media.

Develop a posting schedule and stick to it to maintain engagement with your followers.

- **Share Behind-the-Scenes Content:** Offer your audience a glimpse behind the scenes of your YouTube videos. Share candid photos or videos to provide a more personal and relatable connection with your audience. Contests and giveaways can generate excitement and attract new followers. Use social media to promote and encourage participation in these activities.

- **Collaborate with Influencers:** Working with influencers in your niche can help you reach a larger audience. Collaborative content can introduce your channel to new viewers who share similar interests.

- **Utilize Stories and Live Streams:** Stories and live streams are engaging formats that offer a real-time connection with your audience. Use them to share updates, conduct Q&A sessions, or provide exclusive content.

- **Analyze and Adjust:** Regularly analyze your social media metrics to understand what content resonates most with your audience. Adjust your strategies based on these insights to optimize engagement.

Collaborative Opportunities: Cross-Promoting with Fellow Creators

Cross-promotion with fellow creators is a win-win strategy that benefits all parties involved. Collaborating with other creators exposes your content to their audience and vice versa, allowing you to reach new viewers and diversify your audience. Here are some collaborative opportunities for cross-promotion:

- **Co-Create Videos:** Partner with another creator to co-create a video that showcases both your talents and interests. This collaborative content can attract the attention of both your audiences.

- **Guest Appearances:** Invite other creators to make guest appearances on your channel or be a guest on theirs. This exchange introduces your channels to each other's subscribers.
- **Collaborative Challenges:** Participate in or initiate collaborative challenges that involve multiple creators. This type of content encourages viewers to check out all the creators involved.
- **Feature Each Other's Content:** Give shout-outs or feature each other's content in your videos. Recommending other creators fosters a sense of community and encourages cross-promotion.
- **Collaborate on Social Media:** Host joint live streams or Instagram takeovers with other creators. You can now tap into each other's audiences in real-time.
- **Promote Each Other's Channels:** Cross-promote each other's channels on your respective social media platforms.

Sharing content from fellow creators introduces your audience to new content they might enjoy.

- **Host Collabs with Fans:** Involve your audience in collaborations by featuring fan-generated content or hosting fan-participation events. This fosters a stronger connection between your channel and your community.

- **Collaborate in Niche Communities:** Join niche communities or forums related to your content and collaborate with other creators within those communities.

- **Evaluate Collaborative Success:** After each collaboration, assess its impact on your channel's growth and engagement. Use this information to plan future collaborations with different creators.

By combining these strategies, content creators can increase their visibility, build a loyal audience, and elevate their YouTube channels to new heights.

Chapter 9

Staying Relevant and Adapting to Trends

Staying relevant and adapting to trends are vital factors for content creators seeking long-term success. As the platform evolves, content trends and audience preferences change, requiring creators to be agile and innovative in their approach.

Embracing Change: Navigating YouTube's Evolving Landscape

- **Stay Informed:** Regularly monitor YouTube's updates, algorithm changes, and policy revisions. Being informed about platform developments allows you to adjust your content strategy accordingly.

- **Analyze Audience Insights:** Utilize YouTube's analytics to understand your audience's behavior, preferences, and demographic. This data can assist you in tailoring your content to best suit your viewers.

- **Experiment with New Formats:** Don't be afraid to try out new content formats and styles. Experimenting with different approaches can reveal fresh perspectives and appeal to wider audiences.
- **Listen to Feedback:** Pay attention to feedback from your audience. Whether it's through comments, surveys, or social media, constructive criticism can provide valuable insights for improvement.
- **Evolve with Your Niche:** As your niche evolves, be ready to adapt your content to align with changing trends. Being flexible within your niche ensures that your channel remains relevant and engaging.
- **Quality Over Quantity:** Prioritize the quality of your content over the frequency of uploads. Producing high-quality videos that resonate with your audience has a

more significant impact on staying relevant.

- **Stay Authentic:** While adapting to trends is essential, stay true to your unique voice and brand. Authenticity is a key factor in building a loyal and engaged audience.

Capitalizing on Trends: Seizing Opportunities for Growth

- **Monitor Emerging Trends:** Keep an eye on emerging trends and topics within your niche and beyond. Jumping on early trends can position your content for higher visibility and potential virality.
- **Keyword Research:** Conduct keyword research to identify trending topics and search terms relevant to your content. Optimizing your titles and descriptions for trending keywords can improve discoverability.
- **Trend Analysis:** Analyze the performance of your videos related to

trending topics. Understanding how your audience responds to these trends can guide your future content decisions.

- **React and Respond:** When relevant to your niche, create reaction or response videos to trending content. This can leverage the existing interest in a topic and introduce your channel to a broader audience.

- **Stay Diverse:** Diversify your content to cater to various trending topics and interests. Expanding your content range ensures that you can capture the attention of different audiences.

- **Jump on Social Media Trends:** Utilize social media to identify and participate in trending challenges, hashtags, and conversations. Engaging with social media trends can drive traffic to your YouTube channel.

- **Incorporate Time-Sensitive Content:** Create time-sensitive content related to holidays, events, or special occasions. This type of content has a higher chance of being shared and going viral during specific periods.

- **Be Timely:** Capitalize on trending topics by publishing timely videos. Reacting quickly to emerging trends demonstrates your channel's relevance and ability to stay on top of current events.
- **Balance Evergreen and Trending Content:** While it's essential to embrace trends, also maintain a balance by creating evergreen content that remains relevant and valuable over time.
- **Stay Consistent:** Consistency is key to maintaining relevance on YouTube. Regularly uploading content, engaging with your audience, and staying committed to your niche contribute to your channel's growth.

Chapter 10

Case Studies of YouTube Success

YouTube has become a breeding ground for success stories, with numerous content creators achieving fame, influence, and financial success on the platform. Understanding the strategies and approaches that have led to YouTube's success can provide valuable insights for aspiring content creators and marketers alike.

Analyzing Successful YouTube Channels: Lessons to Learn

- **PewDiePie (Felix Kjellberg):** With over 110 million subscribers, PewDiePie is one of the most successful and influential YouTubers. Key lessons from his success include authenticity, consistent content creation, and engaging directly with his audience through humor and relatable content.

- **Dude Perfect:** This sports and entertainment channel has over 57 million subscribers, and its success lies in creating captivating and impressive trick-shot videos, collaborating with athletes and celebrities, and maintaining a family-friendly image that appeals to a broad audience.
- **Tasty (BuzzFeed):** Tasty's recipe videos have amassed over 45 million subscribers. Their success can be attributed to short and visually appealing recipe demonstrations, catering to quick and easy meal solutions, and adapting their content to various social media platforms.
- **Ryan's World (Ryan Kaji):** Targeting a younger audience, Ryan's World has over 30 million subscribers. Its success lies in creating kid-friendly and educational content, engaging with toys and unboxing videos, and building a brand that extends

beyond YouTube with product lines and licensing deals.

- **Nisha Madhulika:** As a Hindi cooking channel, Nisha Madhulika has achieved tremendous success with over 11 million subscribers. The channel's triumph stems from its authentic approach, clear and step-by-step cooking demonstrations, and catering to the Indian audience's diverse culinary preferences.

Lessons to Learn:

- Consistency: Successful channels consistently produce content, maintaining engagement and loyalty among their audiences.
- Authenticity: Being genuine and relatable fosters a deeper connection with viewers.
- Understanding the Target Audience: Knowing your audience's preferences and interests is crucial for creating relevant content.

- Diversification: Many successful channels diversify their content to reach a broader audience.
- Collaborations: Partnering with other creators can expose your channel to new audiences and foster a sense of community.
- Building a Brand: Developing a strong brand identity can extend beyond YouTube, leading to additional opportunities and revenue streams.

Examining Various Genres: Understanding What Works
- Educational Channels: Channels like Vsauce and CrashCourse have succeeded by offering informative and intellectually stimulating content. Their success is attributed to thorough research, engaging visuals, and clear explanations of complex topics.

- Gaming Channels: Gaming channels like Markiplier and Jacksepticeye have garnered millions of subscribers through their humorous and entertaining gameplay videos. Building a loyal community of viewers who enjoy the creators' personalities and commentary is key to their success.
- Beauty and Fashion Channels: Channels like NikkieTutorials and Jeffree Star have achieved success by providing makeup tutorials, product reviews, and showcasing their unique personalities. High production value, creativity, and staying updated with industry trends are crucial for their growth.
- Travel and Lifestyle Channels: Vloggers like Casey Neistat and FunForLouis have gained a massive following by documenting their travel experiences and lifestyle adventures. Authenticity,

storytelling, and visually captivating content are central to their appeal.

- DIY and Craft Channels: Channels like 5-Minute Crafts and LaurDIY have thrived by offering quick and creative DIY solutions. Their success lies in providing useful and visually engaging content that resonates with a wide audience.

What Works Across Various Genres:

- Engaging Introductions: Captivating viewers from the start is crucial to retain their attention.
- Quality Production: High-quality visuals and audio elevate the overall viewer experience.
- Strong Thumbnails and Titles: Eye-catching thumbnails and compelling titles attract viewers and improve click-through rates.

- Consistent Branding: Building a consistent brand identity strengthens recognition and loyalty.
- Understanding SEO: Using relevant keywords and tags improves discoverability and search rankings.
- Interactivity and Community Engagement: Responding to comments and engaging with the community fosters a loyal fan base.
- Tapping into Trends: Capitalizing on popular trends can expose your content to a broader audience.
- Data-Driven Content Decisions: Analyzing audience data and insights helps optimize content strategy.

Studying successful YouTube channels provides valuable insights into the strategies and tactics that lead to YouTube's success. Emphasizing authenticity, consistency, understanding the target audience, and leveraging trends are common threads across various genres. Additionally, quality production, engaging thumbnails, and strong branding are essential elements of success. By applying the lessons learned from these case studies and understanding what works across different genres, content creators can increase their chances of building thriving YouTube channels and reaching their goals. Remember, YouTube's success is a dynamic process that requires continuous adaptation, improvement, and dedication to creating compelling and valuable content for your audience.

Chapter 11

Why The Majority Of Youtube Channels Don't Succeed

The majority of YouTube channels don't succeed due to various factors and challenges that creators face in the competitive digital landscape.

- **Saturation and Competition:** YouTube is flooded with content across all niches, making it challenging for new channels to stand out and gain visibility amidst fierce competition.

- **Inconsistent Content and Upload Schedule:** Many creators fail to maintain a consistent content schedule, leading to a decline in audience engagement and growth.

- **Lack of Unique Value Proposition:** Channels that don't offer a unique value proposition or fail to differentiate themselves struggle to attract and retain viewers.

- **Expecting Quick Success:** Building a successful channel takes time and dedication. Impatience and unrealistic expectations often lead to disappointment and premature abandonment of the platform.
- **Ignoring Audience Engagement:** Channels that don't engage with their audience, respond to comments or adapt to viewer preferences risk losing viewer loyalty.
- **Quality and Production Issues:** Low-quality videos with poor production value may discourage viewers from subscribing or returning to the channel.
- **Inadequate Promotion and Marketing:** Many creators overlook the importance of promoting their content on social media and other platforms, missing out on potential growth opportunities.

- **Lack of Passion and Consistency:** Channels created solely to make money, without genuine passion for the content, are less likely to succeed in the long run.
- **Failure to Adapt to Algorithm Changes:** YouTube's algorithm evolves regularly, and channels that don't adapt their content strategies may experience a decline in visibility and reach.
- **Monetization Challenges:** Achieving monetization requirements (e.g., 1,000 subscribers and 4,000 watch hours) can be a daunting task, discouraging some creators from continuing their efforts.

Overcoming these challenges requires perseverance, continuous improvement, and a genuine commitment to creating valuable, engaging, and authentic content that resonates with the audience. While success on YouTube is attainable, it demands dedication, innovation, and a willingness to learn from setbacks and grow as a creator.

Chapter 12

Legal and Copyright Considerations

In the digital age, legal and copyright considerations are crucial for content creators to protect their work and avoid potential legal issues. On YouTube, understanding fair use, copyright laws, and licensing music is essential to safeguard your content and build a successful channel.

Understanding Fair Use and Copyright: Protecting Your Content

- Copyright Basics: Copyright is a form of legal protection granted to original works of authorship, including videos, music, images, and text. The moment you create content, it is automatically protected by copyright, and others cannot use it without your permission.
- Fair Use Doctrine: Fair use is a copyright law doctrine that permits for limited use

of copyrighted content without the consent of the copyright owner. It is a nuanced and context-dependent notion that seeks to balance copyright holders' rights while also promoting free expression.

- Fair Use Considerations: When determining fair use, four considerations must be considered: the purpose and character of the use, the nature of the copyrighted work, the amount and substantiality of the portion used, and the effect of the use on the potential market for the copyrighted work.

- Transformative Use: A key consideration in fair use is whether the use is transformative. Transformative use involves adding new meaning, expression, or value to the original work, rather than merely copying or reproducing it.

- Attribution and Credit: Even if you use copyrighted material under fair use, it's essential to provide proper attribution and credit to the original creator. Giving credit shows respect for the creator's work and can help avoid misunderstandings.

- Public Domain: Public domain works are not copyrighted and can be freely used by anybody. Determining whether a work is in the public domain can be complex, so it's essential to verify the status of any material you wish to use.

- Copyright Strikes: Copyright owners can issue copyright strikes against your YouTube channel if they believe you've used their copyrighted material without authorization. Accumulating multiple copyright strikes can result in penalties, including the termination of your channel.

- License Your Content: Licensing your content allows others to use it under specific terms and conditions that you set. By licensing your content, you retain control over how it is used while potentially expanding its reach through others' platforms.

- Protecting Your Content: Take steps to protect your original content by registering it with the relevant copyright office in your country. This can provide additional legal protections in case of copyright disputes.

- Seek Legal Advice: If you're unsure about whether your use of copyrighted material qualifies as fair use or if you encounter legal challenges, seek advice from an attorney experienced in copyright law.

Licensing and Music: Avoiding Copyright Strikes

- Royalty-Free Music: Use royalty-free music for your videos to avoid copyright strikes. Royalty-free music is music that requires a one-time payment or a licensing fee, and you can use it without paying additional royalties for each view.

- YouTube Audio Library: YouTube provides a vast library of free-to-use music that is cleared for use in videos on the platform. Utilizing the YouTube Audio Library ensures that you have the necessary rights to use the music without facing copyright issues.
- Music Licensing Platforms: Consider using music licensing platforms that offer a wide range of tracks for commercial use. These platforms provide affordable licensing options for various uses and often offer high-quality music.
- Original Music: Create your original music or work with musicians and composers to produce custom tracks for your videos. Original music not only ensures copyright compliance but also adds a unique touch to your content.
- Music Libraries: Use music libraries that offer pre-cleared tracks for use in videos. These libraries provide a wide selection of

music, and you can purchase a license for the tracks you want to use.

- Understand Music Licenses: When licensing music, read and understand the terms and conditions of the license. Some licenses may have limitations on the platforms or regions where the music can be used.

- Regularly Check Copyright Status: Copyright status can change over time, so regularly check the copyright status of the music you use in your videos. A song that was previously in the public domain might have regained copyright protection due to changes in copyright laws.

- Give Proper Credit: If you use music that requires attribution, be sure to provide the necessary credit in your video description. Properly crediting the musicians and composers help avoid copyright issues and show respect for their work.

Tips For Creating A Youtube Channel

1. **Create a Google Account:**
   - If you don't have one already, set up a Google Account that will serve as the foundation for your YouTube channel.

2. **Sign in to YouTube and Create the Channel:**
   - Sign in to YouTube with your Google Account.
   - Click on your profile picture and select "Create a channel" from the drop-down menu.
   - Follow the prompts to name your channel and select the appropriate category.

3. **Channel Art and Profile Setup:**
   - Design visually appealing channel art (channel banner and logo) that represents your brand and content.
   - Write an engaging channel description, highlighting what viewers can expect from your channel.

- Plan Your Content Strategy: Create a list of the types of videos you intend to make, such as tutorials, vlogs, reviews, or instructive content.
- Prepare Your Equipment: Purchase basic recording equipment such as a high-quality camera, microphone, and lighting setup. Before submitting your videos, use video editing tools to modify and enhance them.
- Make and Share Your First Video: Plan and script your first video carefully, making sure it fits with the subject of your channel. Shoot the video and edit it, adding any necessary effects or graphics. Upload the video to your channel, along with a catchy title, description, and tags.
- Advertise Your Channel: Share your films on social media and urge your friends and family to subscribe and share them. Collaborate with other YouTubers or influencers to gain more exposure.

- Respond to Comments on Your Videos: Respond to comments on your videos and communicate with viewers to establish a devoted community. To communicate with your audience in real-time, consider holding live streaming or Q&A sessions.
- Analyze and Improve: Use YouTube Analytics to track the performance, demographics, and interaction of your video. To boost the growth of your channel, learn from the data and adapt your content strategy accordingly.
- Stay Consistent and Adapt: Uploading consistently is essential for growing a successful YouTube channel.

Maintain an open mind and change your content based on what your audience appreciates. Keep in mind that creating a great YouTube channel requires time and work. Stay patient, be real, and enjoy the process of developing material that your visitors will appreciate.

CONCLUSION

Finally, "The YouTube Code" provides a new and complete guide to managing the ever-changing terrain of content creation on the world's greatest video-sharing platform. The book includes a treasure mine of practical techniques, insider secrets, and inspirational anecdotes from seasoned YouTuber veterans, empowering prospective creators to turn their passion into a thriving YouTube channel.

The authors underline the value of authenticity and originality throughout the book. They advise people to embrace their individuality and use it to stand out in the cluttered digital landscape. "The YouTube Code" urges producers to go beyond superficial views and focus on establishing a devoted and engaged community by emphasizing the power of storytelling and true connections with the audience.

Finally, "The YouTube Code" is more than just a how-to manual; it is a source of inspiration and empowerment for individuals who want to make their mark in the digital environment. The book urges readers to unlock their creativity and embark on a transforming journey of self-discovery by emphasizing embracing setbacks, experimenting boldly, and persevering through hurdles.

"The YouTube Code" becomes a compass for navigating this dynamic domain in a world where YouTube continues to impact modern entertainment. Aspiring creators will find inside its pages not only the blueprint for success on YouTube, but also for making meaningful connections, leaving a lasting effect, and sharing their authentic voices with a global audience.